◆ ◆ ◆ ◆ ◆

LIFE IN ABUNDANCE

Growing in Courage

◆ ◆ ◆ ◆ ◆

LIFE IN ABUNDANCE

Growing in Courage

by
Peter Gilmour

Saint Mary's Press
Christian Brothers Publications
Winona, Minnesota

Genuine recycled paper with 10% post-consumer waste.
Printed with soy-based ink.

The publishing team included Carl Koch, development editor;
Laurie A. Berg, copy editor; James H. Gurley, production editor
and typesetter; Maurine R. Twait, art director; pre-press, printing,
and binding by the graphics division of Saint Mary's Press.

The acknowledgments continue on page 88.

Printed in the United States of America

Printing: 9 8 7 6 5 4 3 2 1

Year: 2006 05 04 03 02 01 00 99 98

ISBN 0-88489-482-7

◆ ◆ ◆ ◆ ◆

to the memory of
William G. Thompson, SJ (1930–1996)—

Colleague and Friend
in Living and through Dying
always
A Courageous Teacher

Contents

◆ ◆ ◆ ◆ ◆

Jesus said, . . . "I came that [you] may have life, and have it abundantly."

(John 10:7–10)

Jesus' mission is accomplished in each one of us when we nourish the seeds of full life that God has planted in the garden of our soul.

The following story suggests where the task of nurturing the seeds of abundant life needs to begin:

> "I was a revolutionary when I was young and all my prayer to God was 'Lord, give me the energy to change the world.'
>
> "As I approached middle age and realized that half my life was gone without my changing a single soul, I changed my prayer to 'Lord, give me the grace to change all those who come in contact with me. Just my family and friends, and I shall be satisfied.'
>
> "Now that I am an old man and my days are numbered, my one prayer is, 'Lord, give me the grace to change myself.' If I had prayed for this right from the start I should not have wasted my life."
>
> (Bayazid)

Jesus made this point much more saliently: "'Why do you see the speck in your neighbor's eye, but do not notice the log in your own eye? . . . Take the log out of your own eye, and then you will see clearly to take the speck out of your neighbor's eye'" (Matthew 7:3–5).

The meaning of Bayazid's story and Jesus' words is clear: we live life abundantly when we grow in the qualities of character that make life good. These qualities are traditionally called virtues—the inner readiness to do good.

Three Brilliant Flowers: Faith, Hope, Love

In the garden of the soul, faith, hope, and love form the centerpiece. They are essential for living abundantly, living fully. Traditionally called theological virtues, they come as free gifts from God and draw us to God. We cannot earn these qualities; God has already freely planted them in us.

Even so, faith, hope, and love need tending. In prayer we can open our heart, mind, and will to God's grace. We embrace and open ourselves to this grace through reflection and conversation with God about what we believe, how we hope, and the ways we love. When we ponder the Scriptures and examine our beliefs, we nourish faith. When we meditate on the goodness of God's creation, on friendships, and on all God's gifts to us, we nourish hope. When we pray for loved ones, consider how we love, empathize with those needing love, and celebrate the love given to us, we nourish love. As faith, hope, and love spread and grow in the garden of our soul, we truly live life abundantly.

A Harvest of Plenty

The good life of faith, hope, and love is further nurtured as we develop the virtues of courage, justice, prudence, moderation, temperance, forgiveness, and so on. Saint Augustine and other spiritual teachers maintained that these virtues are expressions of faith, hope, and especially love. For instance, in the face of danger to a loved one, people find courage that they never dreamed they had. Living prudently—figuring out what is right in a given situation—becomes easier when love reigns in our heart and focuses our will.

Paradoxically, we find that as we grow in the moral virtues, we also nourish faith, hope, and love in ourselves.

For example, as we grow in justice, we begin to look out for the well-being of other people. In short, we grow more loving. Temperance—creating harmony within ourselves—fosters hopefulness.

Growing a Destiny

Growing abundant life means that we change ourselves by changing the small assertions of self, namely our acts, beginning with an act of prayer. The following wise adage provides a helpful way of thinking about how we can grow in abundance:

> Plant an act; reap a habit.
> Plant a habit; reap a virtue or vice.
> Plant a virtue or vice; reap a character.
> Plant a character; reap a destiny.

Developing our character and our destiny begins with the acts that we plant each day, whether we do them consciously or unconsciously. We give shape to our life by each action we take, day by day. A regular pattern of actions becomes a habit. Eventually our habits determine the shape of our character.

Our character is the combination of our virtues and vices. Our destiny is what finally becomes of us, which depends on the character we build in response to God's grace. A Christlike destiny—life in abundance—begins forming with every act of moral virtue. When we pray to be just, temperate, or moderate, when we pray for courage, honesty, and a forgiving spirit, we acknowledge our dependence on God's grace, but we also give our attention to the development of these qualities of character. Praying for moral virtue is planting, weeding, and watering virtuous acts. The harvest of such prayer will be life lived to the full.

We change the world by changing the small part of it that we are. An old adage says: "Prayer does not change things. Prayer changes people, and people change things." Prayer brings us to the God of love who wants us to have a good life, to live fully, to love, to believe, and to hope. If we open ourselves to God's grace, we will change. Then we can change things.

Praying for Life in Abundance

Virtue, like a garden, fails to thrive without attention and care. Prayer tends the garden. It also allows us to ask for forgiveness so that we can start again when we have left the garden untended. The loving God is always waiting to sustain us and to draw us back to full life. Our God is the God of Hosea who says about sinful and ungrateful Israel: "'I led them with cords of human kindness, with bands of love. I was to them like those who lift infants to their cheeks. I bent down to them and fed them'" (11:4).

Living abundantly leads us frequently to turn the care of the world over to God and to take care of our own soul. To deal with his tendency toward harshness, Vincent de Paul told one of his friends: "I turned to God and earnestly begged him to convert this irritable and forbidding trait of mine. I also asked for a kind and amiable spirit." Vincent's movement of heart toward God involved a surrender to God's presence and power. Vincent knew that living like Christ and clothing himself in Christ's virtues—living abundantly—had to begin with knowledge of his own sins and blessings. Times of prayer, the honest opening and offering of ourselves to God, provide the context for a change of heart, mind, and will to happen.

Praying for the virtues of full life may be roughly compared to tending a garden. "It was a great delight for me," writes Teresa of Ávila, "to consider my soul as a

11

garden and reflect that the Lord was taking a walk in it."
Prayer—the celebration of gratefulness for the goodness
in life—invites God to walk in our garden. Prayer wel-
comes the Master Gardener to plant the seed of virtue
within us. Prayer prepares the soil for the seed when it
opens our fears, doubts, sins, and goodness to the gaze
and grace of the Creator.

In the Epistle to the Ephesians, Paul tells the community to put on God's armor:

> Be strong in . . . the strength of [God's] power.
> . . . Take up the whole armor of God. . . . Fasten
> the belt of truth around your waist, and
> put on the breastplate of righteousness. As shoes
> for your feet put on whatever will make you ready
> to proclaim the gospel of peace. With all of these,
> take the shield of faith.
>
> (6:10–16)

To help us clothe ourselves in the armor of virtue
necessary for a full life, the prayers in this book follow an
ancient pattern: listen *(lectio)*, reflect *(meditatio)*, and
respond *(oratio)*. Here are some suggestions for using the
prayers:

Listen. Each prayer begins with a passage from the
word of God, the wisdom of a spiritual writer, or a story.
Read the passage attentively at least once, or better yet,
several times. Concentrate on one or two sentences that
touch your heart; ponder their meaning for you and their
effect on you. This type of listening is called *lectio divina*,
or "divine studying." The passages are intended to inspire,
challenge, or remind you of some essential aspect of the
virtue.

Reflect. Once you have listened to wisdom, each prayer invites you to reflect on your own experience. This is *meditatio,* or "paying attention." Each reflection can help you attend to how God has been speaking to you in your past and present experience. If you keep a journal, you may want to write your reflections in it. Take the reflection questions with you as you go about your day; ponder them while you drive, wait for an appointment, prepare for bed, or find any moment of quiet.

Respond. Each reflection ends with a prayer of petition and thanks. In *oratio* we ask God for the help we need in nurturing the virtue that helps to form a good life. We should never be shy in asking God for help. After all, Jesus tells us many times to seek God's grace, and he assures us that God's help will come. Indeed, the word *prayer* means "to obtain by entreaty." The petitionary prayer reminds us that we are truly dependent on the goodness and love of God for developing the virtue. The response prayer usually gives thanks for the gifts God has showered upon us already. Giving thanks is another way of waking us up to all the wonders of God's love.

Try reading the prayers aloud. They gain a different feel and power. Or use one line as a prayer throughout the day. Plant the prayer line in your heart as you repeat it while having a cup of coffee, washing your hands, or sitting at your desk.

Starting Points

Create a sacred space. Jesus said, "'When you pray, go to your private room, shut yourself in, and so pray to your [God] who is in that secret place, and your [God] who sees all that is done in secret will reward you'" (Matthew 6:6). Solitary prayer is best done in a place where you can have privacy and silence, both of which can be luxuries in the life of a busy person. If privacy and silence are not possible, create a quiet, safe place within yourself, perhaps while riding to and from work, sitting at the dentist's office, or waiting for someone. Do the best you can, knowing that a loving God is present everywhere.

Move into sacred time. All of time is suffused with God's presence. So remind yourself that God is present as you begin your prayer. If something keeps intruding during your prayer, spend some time talking with God about it. Be flexible, because God's Spirit blows where it will. Gerald May speaks to this when he says:

> The present . . . contains everything that is needed for lovingly beginning the next moment; it seeks only our own willing, responsive presence, just here, just now. . . . There are no exceptions—not in physical pain, not in psychiatric disorder or emotional agony, not in relational strife. . . . Love is too much with us for there to be any exceptions.

Come to prayer with an open mind, heart, and will. Trust that God hears you and wants to support. your desire to nourish the virtues of a good life. Prayer strengthens our will to act. Through prayer God can touch our will and empower us to live according to what we know is true.

Prayer is essential to creating life in abundance because it nourishes the seeds of virtue that are planted in our soul. Listening to wisdom fertilizes the seed. Reflecting on or attending to the virtue waters the seed. Responding with petitionary and thanksgiving prayers shines light on the seed. After reflecting and praying about courage, you will have planted the seed in rich soil

14

so that it can grow. As it grows it will become a bright flower in the garden of your soul.

God be with you as you grow in courage and in living life to the full. You will be a power for the good of us all.

CARL KOCH
Editor

Introduction

Called to Courage

The cowardly lion from *The Wizard of Oz* represents all
of us when he yearns for courage. What this lovable
creature does not realize, however, is that he is already
courageous. Throughout the story his many acts of
courage while protecting his friends are exceptional.
Toward the end of the story, when the lion asks the
cowardly wizard for courage, all the wizard needs to do
is to make the lion aware of his own courage.

The story shows how important courage is to living
life to the full. The cowardly lion suffers from his fears
and doubts. He believes that he is not what he should
be—brave—and that this essential quality of life is miss-
ing from his character.

This children's story—with exceptionally adult
themes—is but a brief glimpse into the wonderful but
sometimes misunderstood virtue of courage. Yes, many
people are more courageous than they at first may think.
No, developing courage is not as easy as drinking a magic
potion. Yes, we are all called to courage. No, we cannot
always expect others to carry the burden of courage. Yes,
a faith community often helps us to act courageously.
No, community may not always be there, so we have to
nourish the virtue within us.

Dramatic Courage

The word *courage* cannot be uttered without thinking of
momentous occasions, without seeing impressive per-
sonages standing up to sordid situations. Remember the
Chinese youth in Tiananmen Square who placed his
slight body in front of the government's gigantic military

tank? Remember Oscar Romero who spoke out forcefully for the poor of his diocese and of the world? Remember Joan of Arc? Remember Thomas Becket, Mahatma Gandhi, Susan B. Anthony, Martin Luther King Jr., Harriet Tubman?

These and so many other exemplars of courage reflect exceptional people in unique situations acting with bravery and valor. Courage. It is the mettle of the heroes and heroines of classical myth. It is manifested by the life and message of Jesus Christ and other progenitors of great religious traditions. It is the distinguishing characteristic of martyrs for faith.

Courage, Day by Day

Another less dramatic but equally important dimension to this Christian moral virtue is the barely noticeable courage expressed in our everyday, ordinary lives. Each day, every day, people meet a host of adversities with courage. Although these situations do not necessarily seem as singular as the more dramatic moments of a Tiananmen Square or a martyrdom for faith, they are, nonetheless, crucibles of courage. Helping a family member, friend, or neighbor in need, speaking up for something one believes in strongly, and learning something difficult are all ordinary challenges of life that can be met with courage.

What Is Courage?

The virtue of courage is the ability, with the grace of God, to choose and do the good, to move toward what is life-giving, in the face of fear, harm, threats, abuse, or even death. The word *courage* comes from the French word *coeur,* meaning "heart." Indeed, courage springs from our heart, our innermost convictions and beliefs.

17

It gives life to our soul and direction to our actions in the face of danger.

Founded in Grace

The promise of Jesus to be with us always is the heart of the virtue of courage. Jesus declared, "'I will not leave you orphaned. . . . The Holy Spirit . . . will teach you everything, and remind you of all that I have said to you. Peace I leave with you; my peace I give to you. . . . Do not let your hearts be troubled, and do not let them be afraid'" (John 14:18,26–27). Over and over, Jesus reassures his followers that he will stand with them in all circumstances. This reassurance flows from his mission to bring life in abundance.

At Pentecost the Apostles finally understood the full power of Jesus' promise. They had been cowering together, fearful of the future. The Spirit fired them with courage. They began to preach fearlessly, and "awe came upon everyone, because many wonders and signs were being done by the apostles" (Acts of the Apostles 2:43).

This same Spirit that en-couraged and empowered the Apostles and the generations of believers since their time is here now, ready to inspire us with courage, too. We do not have to search for the font of courage. The Spirit is always with and in us. Saint Paul speaking to the Roman Christians reminds them, and us, of where we can find unfailing courage:

> Who will separate us from the love of Christ? Will hardship, or distress, or persecution, or famine, or nakedness, or peril, or sword? . . .
>
> No, in all these things we are more than conquerors through him who loved us. For I am convinced that neither death, nor life, nor angels, nor

rulers, nor things present, nor things to come, nor powers, nor height, nor depth, nor anything else in all creation, will be able to separate us from the love of God in Christ Jesus.

(Romans 8:35–39)

Building on Grace

Like all virtues, courage is first empowered by God's grace, but we still build the habit of courage one act at a time. We nurture our courage through the numerous small choices for good that we make. If we cannot do the good in small things, then it is nearly impossible to do the good when faced with daunting opposition. With God's grace we can build our courage. The following are some ways to do so:

The Good

We begin nurturing the seeds of courage by learning about and keeping our heart on the good found in the words of the Scriptures: to love God and love our neighbors as ourselves; to heal the sick; to give drink to the thirsty; to feed the hungry; to act justly, love tenderly, and walk humbly. Each situation in our life asks us to apply these Gospel values.

Knowing and believing in these Gospel values are, of course, not enough. But knowing and believing direct our heart so that when we experience opposition in doing good—in moving toward life—in particular circumstances, we can have courage. Thus, in nurturing the virtue of courage, we need to attend vigilantly to what we believe in.

Years ago a revolutionary professor asked a group of students gathered around him during an informal discussion, "Is there something in your life you would be willing to die for?" An uncomfortable silence hung over the group for what seemed to be a very long time. Finally, someone from the group spoke up, "I think I'd rather know if there is something in your life worth living for?" Now it was the revolutionary's turn to be uncomfortably silent.

Finding our courage asks us to take a look at what we would die for, but also, just as important, what we live for. What "good" do we believe in strongly enough to stand up for it in the face of opposition, pressure, hostility, even danger? And we cannot start attending to the good and figuring out what we believe in during moments of crisis. If a tornado is heading toward our house, it is too late to start digging a basement.

If our hearts are firmly rooted in the good, the values and beliefs of the Gospel, then we are more likely to have courage for the journey's trials. This story is told of a traveler who made a religious pilgrimage:

> An old pilgrim was making his way to the Himalayan Mountains in the bitter cold of winter when it began to rain.
>
> An innkeeper said to him, "How will you ever get there in this kind of weather, my good man?"
>
> The old man answered cheerfully, "My heart got there first, so it's easy for the rest of me to follow."
>
> (Anthony de Mello)

When our heart has a sacred destination, the dangers of the journey become, if not easy, at least less forbidding.

Watching for Inspiration

We need inspiring models of courage. Even though most of us never need to call on ourselves for dramatic courage, we draw courage from those who do act with extraordinary fortitude. Our heroes and heroines are important: they inspire us. People strive to emulate the characteristics of those they admire as they live out their daily life. It is the inspiration that ordinary people receive from extraordinary peoples' heroic actions that motivates each of us to proceed courageously in our everyday affairs.

Clearly, Jesus stands out as a particularly effective model for courage. His willingness to trust God's will over his own, to preach against the excessively institutionalized religious practices of his day, to help the poor and the outcasts, to endure his trial, Passion, and death are all dramatic, courageous moments.

Jesus also exhibited many day-to-day moments of courage. His Apostles tested his courage by questioning him, by wanting a higher place, and by just not getting it at times! Misunderstanding and, at times, hostile listeners tested his courage. One especially significant moment of Jesus' own courage appears in the Gospel of Matthew when a Canaanite woman approaches Jesus to cure her child:

> Jesus left that place and went away to the district of Tyre and Sidon. Just then a Canaanite woman from that region came out and started shouting, "Have mercy on me, Lord, Son of David; my daughter is tormented by a demon." But he did not answer her at all. And his disciples came and urged him, saying, "Send her away, for she keeps shouting after us." He answered, "I was sent only to the lost sheep of the house of Israel." But she came and knelt before him, saying, "Lord, help me." He answered, "It is not fair

21

to take the children's food and throw it to the dogs."
She said, "Yes, Lord, yet even the dogs eat the
crumbs that fall from their masters' table." Then
Jesus answered her, "Woman, great is your faith! Let
it be done for you as you wish." And her daughter
was healed instantly.

(Matthew 15:21–28)

Because of the Canaanite woman's courageous
example, Jesus cures her daughter. By doing so, Jesus
manifests courage in two ways. First, he allows himself
to be taught by a woman, a Canaanite woman, not a customary or comfortable experience in his culture. Second,
he expands his own vision of his ministry beyond the
parochial boundaries of Israel to embrace all humanity.
It is a great turning moment in Jesus' public life, one of
many day-to-day moments of courage manifested in the
Gospels by Jesus and those with whom he interacts.

The Christian tradition is filled with stories of other people who courageously witnessed to faith in Christ—
from Hildegard of Bingen to Martin Luther King Jr.,
from Thomas More to Dorothy Day, from Martin Luther
to Pope John XXIII. They are remembered with special
feasts and prayers and works of art. Many others are
remembered in less formal ways, often by simply telling
the stories of such peoples' lives.

We need our models of courage. By reading the
Gospels and memoirs, and by talking to wise elders and
ordinary good people, we are strengthened.

Claiming Our Fears

Eleanor Roosevelt struggled with shyness for much of
her life. Nevertheless, she won worldwide admiration
for her ability to inspire people to struggle for human
rights and justice. She wrote this about finding courage:
"You gain strength, courage and confidence by every

22

experience in which you really stop to look fear in the face. You are able to say to yourself, 'I lived through this horror. I can take the next thing that comes along.' . . . You must do the thing you think you cannot do."

Ironically, to nurture our courage, we must—like Eleanor Roosevelt—accept our fears, otherwise they will defeat us throughout our life. Jesus wanted his followers to put aside their fears because, of course, he understood them. He knew that their fear would trap them and corrupt their soul—would sap them of life. Again he gave them an example of facing fear. His agony in the Garden of Gethsemane was real. Various translations describe Jesus feeling "distressed and agitated" (NRSV); "horror and anguish" (RSV); "troubled and distressed" (NAB). His way of coping was to offer these fears to God in complete honesty and faith.

Nowhere do the Scriptures say that God miraculously took away all Jesus' fears, but Jesus faced his torture and death with courage. Fear will come and go, but without facing fear and confronting it, God's grace cannot free us from its control—so we will be victims of it. As Rollo May says, "If we were not able to be aware of ourselves, we would be pushed along by instinct or the automatic march of history, like bees or mastodons." Courageous people are afraid, but their fear does not prevent them from doing good, from moving toward what gives life.

Taking Steps

Courage, like other virtues, does not exist by itself. It must be embodied in action. It is through specific instances of courageous action that we first come in contact with this virtue. At times we experience courageous action firsthand through another person's example. Other times we hear about courageous action through stories. We begin to realize that what we admire in others is also possible within our own behavior.

This realization comes easily; moving that realization to action is much more difficult. As Eleanor Roosevelt makes clear though, we need to begin with the small acts of courage. Sometimes small acts of courage have dramatic results. Jackie Robinson's breaking of the color barrier in baseball provides the following example of courage:

> The Brooklyn Dodgers' owner, Branch Rickey, told Robinson, "It'll be tough on you. You are going to take a lot of abuse, be ridiculed, and receive more verbal punishment than you ever thought possible." Rickey continued, "But I'm willing to back you all the way if you have the determination to make it work."
>
> In short order, Robinson experienced Rickey's gloomy prediction. He was abused verbally and physically as players intentionally ran him over and ran him down. The crowd was quick with racial slurs and deriding comments. Opponents, as well as his own teammates, ridiculed Robinson.
>
> Around mid-season, Robinson was having a particularly horrendous day. He had fumbled several grounders, overthrown first base, and batted poorly. The crowd that day was especially nasty. Then something miraculous happened. In front of this critical crowd, Pee Wee Reese, the team captain, walked over from his shortstop position and put his arm around Jackie Robinson.
>
> Robinson later reflected, "That simple gesture saved my career. Pee Wee made me feel as if I belonged."

Jackie Robinson provides a dramatic profile in courage, but the modest act of courage of Pee Wee Reese sustained

Robinson. No doubt it also sustained Reese's sense of his own integrity.

We foster our own courage by taking steps into the unknown, performing the small acts of courage that are offered to us by life.

$\mathscr{A}$nd So We Pray

Through the deep and patterned reflection that prayer has to offer, we may move courage from idea to action in our own life. This is the reason for meditating with these reflections on courage. This is the opportunity to become the hero or heroine of our own life.

We pray for courage should we find ourselves in a momentous situation requiring great nobility and valor. We also pray for courage as a staple in our everyday affairs. These reflections can move us toward both of these goals. They reflect the courageous attitudes and behaviors of others so that we may be inspired by their example, imitate their behavior, and, in turn, inspire others by our own courageous actions.

And so we pray:

Living God,
Happy those whose strength is in you;
they have courage to make the pilgrimage!
As they go through the Valley of the Weeper,
they make it a place of springs,
clothed in generous growth by early rains.
They make their way from strength to strength,
soon to see God in Zion.

. . . .

For you, God, are a sun and shield,
bestowing grace and glory.

(Psalm 84:5–11)

Exodus Experiences

Listen

Though Moses never did quite agree to go, he went, albeit reluctantly. He went to Pharaoh and spoke the word of God, "Let my people go!" We know the rest of the story—a story taken by oppressed people down through history as their story. Generations of people have taken courage, found strength, and discovered hope for their own liberation through the exodus of the Hebrews from their captivity. The cry of Moses to "let my people go" has become the battle cry for those of every age in bondage.

(Jim Wallis)

◆　◆　◆　◆　◆

Reflect

Moses did lead the Israelites out of Egypt, but he took a lot of convincing. When God first called him to be the leader of the Exodus, Moses tried to back out. He asked God: "'Who am I that I should go to Pharaoh, and bring the Israelites out of Egypt?'" (Exodus 3:11); "'Suppose they do not believe me or listen to me?'" (Exodus 4:1). When God reassured Moses on those issues, Moses said, "'I have never been eloquent, . . . I am slow of speech and slow of tongue'" (Exodus 4:10). God even helped Moses with this problem by prompting Aaron to speak for him. Finally, Moses ran out of excuses. God gave him help. Moses found his courage.

What situations in your life demand courage; that is, in what situations do you want to move toward the good, toward what is life-giving, but your fears, like Moses', keep getting in the way? Call on God to give you the grace and understanding that you need to move from bondage to freedom.

Respond

God of Moses, my God, you told us that you are "making all things new" (Revelation 21:5). Make my heart newly courageous to face my fears, so that I can not only be free from what binds me but can free my sisters and brothers who languish in bondage.

Keeping Faith

Listen

In spite of everything I still believe that people are really good at heart. I simply can't build up my hopes on a foundation consisting of confusion, misery, and death. I see the world gradually being turned into a wilderness, I hear the ever-approaching thunder, which will destroy us too. I can feel the sufferings of millions and yet, if I look up into the heavens, I think that it will all come right, that this cruelty too will end, and that peace and tranquility will return again.

In the meantime, I must uphold my ideals, for perhaps the time will come when I shall be able to carry them out.

(Anne Frank)

◆　◆　◆　◆　◆

Reflect

How is it possible to be optimistic in the face of over-whelming evil? How is it possible to believe in a peaceful future amid present strife? How is it possible to stay true to one's ideals when faced with the reality of pain and suffering? Looking up to the heavens, as did Anne Frank, requires not only faith but courage. It is difficult not to give in to the day-to-day manifestations of evil. It is hard not to accept the party line. It is frustrating not to live for the moment. Dreams of a redeemed world rely on the courage to embrace a positive outlook on life and a willingness to pursue a better future.

Talk with God about the ideals or values that you find hardest to uphold in the present time. Ask for the courage you need to do the good.

Respond

God of strength, help me to remember Paul's words to the Romans and to me: "We know that all things work together for good for those who love God" (Romans 8:28). Even though I do not see how taking some small steps toward the good can make a positive difference in our troubled world, I want to take courage from these words. Turn my small steps into the seeds of goodness.

The Passage of Time

Listen

It has never been easy for me to understand the obliteration of time, to accept, as others seem to do, the swelling and corresponding shrinkage of seasons or the conscious acceptance that one year has ended and another begun. There is something here that speaks of our essential helplessness and how the greater substance of our lives is bound up with waste and opacity. Even the sentence parts seize on the tongue, so that to say "Twelve years passed" is to deny the fact of biographical logic. How can so much time hold so little, how can it be taken from us?

(Carol Shields)

◆ ◆ ◆ ◆ ◆

Reflect

We need courage to look at our own life, not in a nostal-
gic way but in honest, reflective self-assessment. Are we
willing to admit that the past is history, the present is
opportunity, and the future is prayer?

Recall a particular twelve-year period from your
own life. What were some instances of courage and cow-
ardice during that portion of your life? What would you
like to see happen in the next twelve years of your life?
What sort of courage will you need to build, plant, and
create your future?

Respond

Living God, may I sustain my courage with a dose of your
realism:

For everything there is a season, and a time for every
matter under heaven:
    a time to be born, and a time to die;
    a time to plant, and a time to pluck up what is
        planted;

    . . . .

    a time to seek, and a time to lose;
    a time to keep, and a time to throw away;
    a time to tear, and a time to sew;
    a time to keep silence, and a time to speak;
    a time to love, and a time to hate;
    a time for war, and a time for peace.
                          (Ecclesiastes 3:1–8)

The Power of God

Listen

"Be strong and of good courage. Do not be afraid or dismayed before the king of Assyria and all the horde that is with him; for there is one greater with us than with him. With him is an arm of flesh; but with us is the LORD our God, to help us and to fight our battles." The people were encouraged by the words of King Hezekiah of Judah.

(2 Chronicles 32:7–8)

◆ ◆ ◆ ◆ ◆

Reflect

The whole history of the people of Israel is one long tale of God coming to their rescue in times of trouble. King Hezekiah's words could just as readily apply to us, "with us is the LORD our God." Although many of our everyday battles are not military in nature, nonetheless we face opposition frequently in other activities and endeavors.

What are the battles you fight in your own life? Who is it that speaks encouraging words to you, reminds you of God's presence, admonishes you to be fearless? Thank God for those who give you courage, and ask God for strength in your daily battles.

Respond

God, I pray for the courage to enter into controversy and conflict always considering your ever-abiding life and love. Let me never forget your promise always to aid and assist me regardless of the difficulty at hand. In particular, today I need courage in this struggle . . .

Seeds of Courage

Listen

We must "walk the rocky hillside sowing clover" . . . we must. Each of us, in spite of the dark or the danger, we must pocket our seeds and go out into the night. It is where we claim the significance of our lives. In spite of everything that would reduce our power, we must sow our seeds, build our families, dignify our work, enflesh our dreams and keep our promises. We must make bread, vigils, petitions, laws, friendships, treaties, babies, dances and worship. We must believe that the darkest aspects of our humanness contain the seeds of transformation. We must resist our lack of hope, our loss of life. We must finger our very lives and times as prayer beads, sow them on the rocky hillside.

(Miriam Theresa MacGillis)

◆ ◆ ◆ ◆ ◆

Reflect

People, things, events can easily get us down. At times they can overwhelm us. We can fall into inaction and depression. It takes courage in the face of such obstacles to sow seeds, to enflesh dreams, to keep promises. Such courage has roots firmly planted in the soil of the virtues of faith and hope. In taking courageous steps, we nourish faith and hope. Building on God's grace for faith and hope nourishes our courage.

What are the seeds you find yourself ready to sow? What dreams do you want to make happen? What promises do you want to keep? And where will you find the courage to move ahead? What beads from your life, what past acts of courage, can you finger as prayer beads, strengthening you?

Respond

Creator God, guide and strengthen me as I follow your lead in trying to sow the seeds of new life in the world as it is. Please keep my hope alive, my faith firm, and my courage sharp, so that even when the seeds of your word fall on rocky ground or shallow soil, I do not fall prey to despair. May I continually give you thanks for my courageous acts and go forth to sow on good soil where people "'hear the word and accept it and bear fruit'" (Mark 4:20).

Going Into That Good Night

Listen

Of the people I have watched fight terminal disease, most faced death as they had life. Some accepted the verdict with bitterness and silence as if dying was just one more final addition to a lifetime list of failures. Others went with shouts of joy, their eyes turned to a vision of Jesus coming down to retrieve them. Others raged and fought to the last breath, either afraid of dying, reluctant to leave such good times, or not satisfied with what they had yet done on earth.

(Tim McLaurin)

◆ ◆ ◆ ◆ ◆

Reflect

Death is a great equalizer, ultimately sparing no one. When, where, and under what circumstances we will die remain a mystery for most of us. To think about our own death is difficult. To watch others die, particularly loved ones who are close to us, is sometimes more difficult. Understanding how to be with the dying, how to comfort them, how to talk with them, and how to be of assistance to them demand courage. Part of the reason that we need courage at these times is that we are confronted with our own mortality too. Indeed, fear of death can make cowards of most of us.

Look at the way you live right now. Will your way of life prepare you to die with hope and courage or with dread and fear? What thoughts about your own mortality does being close to someone who is dying trigger in you?

Respond

Eternal God, may I always be moved to courage as I pray with Paul:

> "For we know that if the earthly tent we live in is destroyed, we have a building from God, a house not made with hands, eternal in the heavens. . . .
> From now on, therefore, we regard no one from a human point of view. . . . If anyone is in Christ, there is a new creation: everything old has passed away; see, everything has become new!"
> (2 Corinthians 5:1,16–17)

A Teacher Named Anger

Listen

Anger is fuel. We feel it and we want to do something. Hit someone, break something, throw a fit, smash a fist into the wall, tell those bastards. But we are *nice* people, and what we do with our anger is stuff it, deny it, bury it, block it, hide it, lie about it, medicate it, muffle it, ignore it. We do everything but *listen* to it.

Anger is meant to be listened to. Anger is a voice, a shout, a plea, a demand. Anger is meant to be respected. Why? Because anger is a *map*. Anger shows us what our boundaries are, and it shows us where we want to go. Anger lets us see where we've been and lets us know when we haven't liked it. Anger points the way, not just the finger. In the recovery of a blocked artist, anger is a sign of health.

Anger is meant to be acted upon. It is not meant to be acted out. Anger points the direction. We are meant to use anger as fuel to take the actions we need to move where our anger points us. With a little thought, we can usually translate the message that our anger is sending us.

(Julia Cameron)

◆ ◆ ◆ ◆ ◆

Reflect

What situations have recently made you angry? Step back, get centered, and listen to what is deep within your seethings and your outbursts. How is courage needed to be willing to face your anger? How can you turn your anger into courage to do the good?

Using these specific examples as centerpoints for reflection takes courage. First, we need to admit that we are angry people at times. Second, we need to concentrate on parts of ourselves that many of us would like to either ignore or forget. Last, we need to be still and calm in the face of our anger in order to learn from it. These actions can be fueled by anger. For sure, this is hard work. But the rewards of facing our anger, learning from it, and moving on from it is worthwhile activity that nurtures courage.

Respond

Loving God, make me an instrument of your peace. Where there is hatred, let me sow love. Where there is injury, pardon; where there is doubt, faith; where there is despair, hope; where there is darkness, light; where there is sadness, joy. O Divine Teacher, grant that I may not so much seek to be consoled as to console; to be understood as to understand; to be loved as to love. For it is in giving that we receive; it is in pardoning that we are pardoned; and it is in dying that we are born to eternal life.

(Peace Prayer of Francis of Assisi)

Inside Ourselves

Listen

Through compassion it is possible to recognize that the craving for love that men feel resides also in our own hearts, that the cruelty that the world knows all too well is also rooted in our own impulses. Through compassion we also sense our hope for forgiveness in our friend's eyes and our hatred in their bitter mouths. When they kill, we know that we could have done it; when they give life, we know that we can do the same. For a compassionate man nothing human is alien: no joy and no sorrow, no way of living and no way of dying.

(Henri J. M. Nouwen)

◆ ◆ ◆ ◆ ◆

Reflect

Taking a deep look inside ourselves requires courage because tremendous opportunities for action, both good and ill, reside within us all. What we choose to do is in large measure who we are; who we are helps us to determine what we choose to do. It is easy to see how this capacity for both good and bad gets played out in others. It's much harder to come into contact with this same reality within ourselves. It is a courageous step to admit that within ourselves is the potential both for good and for evil. Nevertheless, we gain courage when we realistically look at what we are capable of and then take the steps to do the good of which we are capable.

What acts of compassion have you done recently? Who needs your compassion now? Ask God for the courage you will need to show compassion for people who are different from you, for those in trouble, and for your enemies.

Respond

God, who through Jesus Christ gave us a model of courageous compassion, help me to become more and more sensitive to both myself and other people. I pray for the courage to be compassionate toward those who have caused me harm, especially . . .

A Thirst for Justice

Listen

I came to St. Thomas as part of a reform movement in the Catholic Church, seeking to harness religious faith to social justice. In 1971, the worldwide synod of bishops had declared justice a "constitutive" part of the Christian gospel. When you dig way back into Church teachings, you find that this focus on justice has been tucked in there all along in "social encyclicals." Not exactly coffee-table literature. The documents have been called the best-kept secret of the Catholic Church. And with good reason. The mandate to practice social justice is unsettling because taking on the struggles of the poor invariably means challenging the wealthy and those who serve their interests. "Comfort the afflicted and afflict the comfortable"—that's what Dorothy Day, a Catholic social activist, said is the heart of the Christian gospel.

(Helen Prejean)

◆ ◆ ◆ ◆ ◆

ℛeflect

Helen Prejean, the author of *Dead Man Walking*, challenged all of us to reflect on punishment, the need to forgive, and the injustices in society that breed crime. Like most courageous, prophetic voices, Sister Helen has been pilloried by her critics. Nevertheless, she reminds us that religion's Achilles' heel is the tendency to become inward-looking, taking care of their own exclusively, ignoring the broader issues of injustice. When this happens, churches take on the trappings of a country club or cult. For a church to focus its attention outward, on the poor and disadvantaged people of the community, is a courageous act. A church, of course, is people, and how each one of us participates in the mission of social justice is a vital question to consider.

How do you reach out to the poor and disadvantaged people in your own life? What interior and exterior opposition might you encounter if you took a more active role in caring for needy people or in struggling against injustice? These are difficult questions to be answered courageously.

ℛespond

Gracious God, may I be challenged and given courage by these words:

> Bear one another's burdens, and in this way you will fulfill the law of Christ. . . . God is not mocked, for you reap whatever you sow. . . . So let us not grow weary in doing what is right, for we will reap at harvest time, if we do not give up.
>
> (Galatians 6:2–9)

Expanding Horizons

Listen

My church and my Christian faith were at the heart of my continuing search but did not confine it. I found new insights from others outside, who brought different visions that enriched and illuminated my own way. At a time when I felt stuck in a sort of spiritual bog, my writer-teacher friend Marcie Hershman urged me to try again to read Martin Buber's *I and Thou*, a book I had found too formidable when I first tried it a few years before, but on this new attempt it seemed to open to me. I felt renewed by the profound spiritual vision of the great scholar of Judaism; the sometimes painful changes I experienced through the passages of my own journey were illuminated in Buber's eloquent words: "Creation happens to us, burns itself into us, recasts us in burning—we tremble and are faint, we submit. We take part in creation, meet the creator, reach out to him, helpers and companions."

I did not want my own companions in this greatest of all journeys to be limited to members of my own church or faith, even though others had different rituals and rules for serving and finding God.

(Dan Wakefield)

◆ ◆ ◆ ◆ ◆

Reflect

Insights into the quest for God, the meaning of life,
and how to live in community come from a variety of
sources. It's easy to settle into a rut, to assume that what
we already know is enough, to presume that one church
has a total monopoly on insight. It takes courage to expand our education and extend our horizons, but taking
these steps toward the good also expands our courage.

What readings have challenged you recently to better understand what the life of faith is all about? What
other voices have you heard outside your own customary
religious tradition that bespoke of God? What steps
toward growing in faith will give you a deeper understanding of the good?

Respond

Let your steadfast love come to me, O God,
your salvation according to your promise.
So shall I have an answer for those who reproach me,
for I trust in your words.
Leave the word of truth in my mouth—
for in your decree is my hope.

(Psalm 119:41–43)

An Argument with God

Listen

I have never renounced my faith in God. I have risen against His justice, protested His silence and sometimes His absence, but my anger rises up within faith and not outside it. I admit that this is hardly an original position. It is part of Jewish tradition. But in these matters I have never sought originality. On the contrary, I have always aspired to follow in the footsteps of my father and those who went before him. Moreover, the texts cite many occasions where prophets and sages rebelled against the lack of divine interference in human affairs during times of persecution. Abraham and Moses, Jeremiah and Rebbe Levi-Yitzhak of Berdichev teach us that it is permissible for man to accuse God, provided it be done in the name of faith in God. If that hurts, so be it. Sometimes we must accept the pain of faith so as not to lose it. And if that makes the tragedy of the believer more devastating than that of the nonbeliever, so be it. To proclaim one's faith within the barbed wire of Auschwitz may well represent a double tragedy, of the believer and his Creator alike.

(Elie Wiesel)

◆ ◆ ◆ ◆ ◆

Reflect

The genocide perpetrated in the concentration camps was a tragedy of faithlessness. Many day-to-day situations tempt us to other sorts of faithlessness. As Wiesel points out, the Bible is filled with instances in which prophets and psalmists accuse God of not helping them overcome the enemies of their faith. Even Jesus cried from the cross, "My God, my God, why have you deserted me?" These kinds of lamentation demand faith in a God who really does listen to and love us but whose ways we cannot ever completely understand. In the process of declaring our wants, anger, hurt, and frustration, we invite God to give us the courage we need to continue living faithfully.

Offer your lamentations to God about situations in which you feel powerless and abandoned by God's grace and courage. Thank God for times when you have had courage in the face of temptations to faithlessness.

Respond

My God, my God, why have you deserted me?
Far from my prayer, from the words I cry?

. . . .

Yet, Holy One,

. . . .

In you our ancestors put their trust;
they trusted and you rescued them.

(Psalm 22:1–4)

In the Face of Danger

Listen

I had vaguely heard of liberation theology and the movement of worker priests, but I knew nothing of the militant Church, the thousands and thousands of Christians dedicated to serving those most in need with humility and anonymity. They formed a part of the only organization with the ability to help the victimized, the Vicaria de la Solidaridad, an entity created for that purpose by the cardinal during the first days of the dictatorship [in Chile]. For seventeen years, a large group of priests and nuns would risk their lives to save others and to report crimes. It was a priest who showed me the safest routes to political asylum. Some of the people I helped leap over a wall ended up in France, Germany, Canada, and the Scandinavian countries, all of which accepted hundreds of Chilean refugees. Once I had started down that road, it was impossible to turn back, because one case led to another and then another . . . and there I was, committed to various underground activities, hiding or transporting people, passing on for publication in Germany information others had obtained about the tortured or disappeared, and taping interviews with victims in order to establish a record of everything that happened in Chile, a task more than one journalist took on in those days.

(Isabel Allende)

◆ ◆ ◆ ◆ ◆

Reflect

Most of us will probably never find ourselves in such dire circumstances as did Isabel Allende when the military dictatorship murdered her uncle, the elected president of Chile, and began the systematic brutalization of any dissenter. Yet we live in a world where unjust governmental activity is commonplace. Allende's models of courage were women and men who in other circumstances might never have had to place their life in jeopardy, but under oppression risked their life for their sisters and brothers.

Whom do you admire as models of courage in the face of injustice? What have you learned from these models of courage? What steps can you put into practice to rectify situations of injustice, keeping in mind the adage, "think globally, act locally"?

Respond

Just God, give me courage to follow my models of courage. May I take to heart Jesus' words: "'You are the salt of the earth; but if salt has lost its taste, how can its saltiness be restored? . . . You are the light of the world. . . . Let your light shine'" (Matthew 5:13–16). Keep me salty and filled with shining light.

Do I Believe?

Listen

Truth can be frightening because it is a revisitation of meanings we wished to forget, realities we had long ago buried inside us. When the Jews gathered at Mount Sinai to hear God's word, after slavery, after the terror of the Egyptian experience, the revelation was not only for the people as a whole, but for each individual to recognize his or her own truth inside of God's words. Each one must learn in his or her own life how to bring forth words that are true and come from deep inside—this, too, is part of God's revelation.

(David J. Wolpe)

◆ ◆ ◆ ◆ ◆

Reflect

This is extraordinarily hard work. Some people prefer to leave the courageous search for God's revelation solely to other spiritual authorities—their church, synagogue, or mosque. "Just tell me what to believe," they say. Yet each person, whether an active participant in a religious tradition or not, must come to grips with her or his own life, come to grips with her or his place in God's word and world. And that's not all. Everyone can also courageously share their insights with others. We all participate in God's life by finding the words to speak about God's unique revelation to each one of us. Yes, it is not only extraordinarily hard work, but also a courageous act.

We nurture courage by finding the good and keeping our eyes fixed on it when confronted with difficult choices. Compose a brief mission statement for yourself that expresses succinctly what you believe, what you would stand up for even in the face of danger.

Respond

God, we pray for the courage to find you in all things. We also pray for the courage to find the words to speak about where we have found you. Help us to share your myriad presences in this world with others.

In the Face of Evil

Listen

But when they crossed through the traffic of the round-about his gaze fell level with the Plaza where upward of fifty women were walking in a slow, ritualistic procession. Each wore a white scarf which bound them together in some as yet unknown sorority. Were it not for the scarves they could have been a cross section of the city's women: some clearly middle class, who could have been his neighbors; some poor Indians whose skin shone like polished wood. They all carried signs so that at a distance they appeared like a gathering of religious zealots brandishing cryptic phrases from the Book of Revelations, advertising the apocalypse.

As soon as he and Esme reached the edge of the Plaza he understood that the signs were epitaphs and that the women were bound by motherhood. Photographs of the disappeared were centered in each sign, and beneath them were inscriptions written in large black letters:

Where is Ruben Macias?
Where is Julia Obregon?
Have you taken my daughter and grandson?

As the women moved silently past he could almost hear the anguish of their questions, but that imagined sound was less affecting than the faces of the mothers and those who'd vanished from their lives.

(Lawrence Thornton)

◆ ◆ ◆ ◆ ◆

Reflect

How does one explain a small group of women moved
to courageous acts in the face of injustice—in this case
the disappearances and executions of their children in
Argentina during military rule? Surely they knew the
danger in which they were putting themselves. Surely
these women knew that they themselves could be the
next victims of government repression. Yet they went
ahead and publicly proclaimed the injustice that made
their loved ones disappear. Their love gave them courage
to act. Such action is often the stuff of saints' lives. But
saints, like the marching women, are ordinary people
doing extraordinary things at difficult moments in life.

What ordinary people do you see facing difficulties
with courage? Talk to God about facing your ordinary
problems with similar fortitude.

Respond

God, give me the courage to challenge evil wherever it is
present. Help me witness to goodness every day of my
life.

Assuming Leadership

Listen

After the death of Moses the servant of the LORD, the LORD spoke to Joshua son of Nun, Moses' assistant, saying, "My servant Moses is dead. Now proceed to cross the Jordan, you and all this people, into the land that I am giving to them, to the Israelites. . . . As I was with Moses, so I will be with you; I will not fail you or forsake you. . . . Only be strong and very courageous, being careful to act in accordance with all the law that my servant Moses commanded you. . . . This book of the law shall not depart out of your mouth; you shall meditate on it day and night, so that you may be careful to act in accordance with all that is written in it. For then you shall make your way prosperous, and then you shall be successful. I hereby command you: Be strong and courageous; do not be frightened or dismayed, for the LORD your God is with you wherever you go."

(Joshua 1:1–9)

◆ ◆ ◆ ◆ ◆

Reflect

God gave Moses the courage to lead the people to the Jordan River; now Joshua receives both the mandate from God and also the courage. The words that God speaks to Joshua are virtually the same words that the risen Christ spoke to the disciples as he sent them out to spread the Good News: "'I am with you always, to the end of the age'" (Matthew 28:20). God calls us all to assume the mantle of discipleship and gives us the courage to do so.

What "rivers" are you being asked to lead people across? How are you being called to courageously assume the mantle of discipleship? If you need reassurance, pray repeatedly Christ's words, "'I am with you always.'"

Respond

God of my ancestors in the faith, when I weaken in the face of opposition, my own fears, hostility, or doubt, may I remember that the words you spoke to Joshua are also your words to me: "Be strong and bold, . . . I will be with you" (Deuteronomy 31:23).

Ideally Real; Really Ideal

Listen

In Zen it is said that the gap between accepting things the way they are and wishing them to be otherwise is "the tenth of an inch of difference between heaven and hell." If we can accept whatever hand we've been dealt—no matter how unwelcome—the way to proceed eventually becomes clear. This is what is meant by right action: the capacity to observe what's happening and act appropriately, without being distracted by self-centered thoughts. If we rage and resist, our angry fearful minds have trouble quieting down sufficiently to allow us to act in the most beneficial way for ourselves and others.

(Phil Jackson)

◆　◆　◆　◆　◆

Reflect

It is hard to keep facing ourselves. It is so easy to put the blame on others, to live life in some artificial, unreal zone, to deny who we are. To accept the reality of our life is a courageous act. Once we make this step, we then can accept who we are and what we can do. The process of stepping over this gap gives us vision. It opens doors to right action for ourselves and for others.

Name the two aspects of yourself that you find most hard to accept, the things that you fear the most about yourself. Then enter into a dialog with each of these fearful aspects; confront them, but claim them as your own.

Respond

That I may be able to see myself as I really am, that I may accept myself and develop my God-given strengths and talents, I pray to you, living God. Hear my prayer that I may learn right action.

God at My Side

Listen

God's spirit entered Obed's son Azariah. Meeting Asa, he said, "Listen closely, Asa, and Judah and Benjamin as well: God is with you when you abide with God. Seeking, you will find God, but if you desert God, God will desert you. Israel lived godlessly for far too long, and they abandoned the law and traditions. Only when they found themselves in trouble did they turn back to the God of Israel. They searched for and found their God again. During their time of godlessness, life was dangerous, chaotic, and confused. Peoples fought with one another. So, you have courage. Strengthen your heart and hand because God will reward your efforts.

(Adapted from 2 Chronicles 15:1–7)

♦ ♦ ♦ ♦ ♦

Reflect

Living with God demands courage. When things go well, it is easy to assume God is with us. But when things go poorly, doubts arise. God never really abandons us, but we forget God's constant presence. And we pay the consequences of anxiety, confusion, distress—not because God wants this but because these are the natural results of turning away from God's truth, God's way, and God's life, all of which require courage.

Do you find yourself abandoning God during hard times? Do you seek God only in times of extreme need, or do you nurture your faith and courage all along the way by nurturing your relationship with God?

Respond

God, your faithfulness to the people of Israel stands both as testimony and as promise. Help us to take courage from your mighty witness and generous promise to be always with us. Give us the courage always to be present to you, to seek you, and to be with you.

Art and the Artist

Listen

I've to make these canastitas [small baskets] my own way and with my song in them and with bits of my soul woven into them. If I were to make them in great numbers there would no longer be my soul in each, or my songs. Each would look like the other with no difference whatever and such a thing would slowly eat up my heart. Each has to be another song which I hear in the morning when the sun rises and when the birds begin to chirp and the butterflies come and sit down on my baskets so that I may see a new beauty, because, you see, the butterflies like my baskets and the pretty colors on them, that's why they come and sit down, and I can make my canastitas after them.

(B. Traven)

◆ ◆ ◆ ◆ ◆

Reflect

This basket weaver refuses to compromise his artistic integrity. He feels strongly and deeply about his creativity. He is not willing to surrender his artistic beliefs and behaviors in order to mass produce his *canastitas,* to make more money. He courageously believes in his own artistic integrity.

Into what activities in your own life do you weave bits of your soul? Into what do you put your own song? And how do you find the courage to keep these beautiful songs of the soul alive and well in your daily activities?

Respond

God, you are the supreme artist, weaving your presence into the fabric of our life. Give me the courage to emulate your divine presence by exercising my own artistic integrity in all that I do. Help me to manifest your presence in all that I do. I ask for the strong heart of you, my Creator.

Heroines and Heroes

Listen

The word "hero" may bother some of us because we have become accustomed to using it only for those who stand out the farthest and the most. The Gandhis, the Churchills, the Martin Luther Kings, the Mother Teresas—*they're* the heroes. We're just plain folks. But even as we say that, we know it isn't true. Granted, we may not have reached the pinnacle of heroism they have; nonetheless, each of us nurtures in her heart a secret account of how heroic we have been, and each of us has a story we tell ourselves about how we have lived our lives, a private scenario in which *we* are the heroes.

(Dick Westley)

◆ ◆ ◆ ◆ ◆

Reflect

Who are your heroes and heroines? Maybe they are as familiar as a family member or a neighbor. Maybe they are as different as people from another ethnic or racial group or from another country. Maybe they are from another time in history. What is it about each of them that is courageous? Let's not stop there, however. Let's put ourselves into this picture.

Who do you think looks upon you as their heroine or hero? What qualities in you might they admire? What would they see as courageous in you? But let's not stop there either. Recall stories of your own heroism. When have you been a hero to yourself? What are the courageous elements to your own stories of heroism?

Respond

God, help me to hold those I admire in my heart. Give me the eyes to see and the ears to hear goodness and courage in the famous personalities and in the ordinary people with whom I live and work. Give me the courage also to see the heroic in myself.

Who Are My Sisters and Brothers?

Listen

A man had been wandering in the forest for several days unable to find a way out. Finally he saw another man approaching. He asked him, "Brother, will you please tell me the way out of the forest?" Said the other, "I do not know the way out either, for I too have been wandering here for many days. But this much I can tell you. The way that I have gone is not the way."

So it is with us. We know that the way we have been going is not the way. Now let us join hands and look for the way together.

(Rabbi Hayyim of Zans)

◆ ◆ ◆ ◆ ◆

Reflect

What are the "forests" of our own life? How do we find
our way out of them? First, we have to recognize that we
don't know the way. Second, we often have to ask for
help. And when we do ask for help, we need to realize
that the other person might not be able to help us as
thoroughly and completely as we would like. Each of
these steps takes courage. But the ultimate step, joining
hands with another, is perhaps the most courageous step
of all. To trust ourselves, to trust others, and to trust the
relationship that flows from the joining of hands is no
easy task.

What forests might you find a way out of with the
help of someone else? If you need courage to reach out
for help, ask God's help with it.

Respond

When we come into contact with people different from
ourselves, when we are in strange and unfamiliar situations, when we see people who haven't had all the advan-
tages that we have had, when we are in tense situations,
gracious God, give us courage to join hands with them.

$\mathcal{F}$earful Moments

$\mathcal{L}$isten

When I was asked to go to Uganda to establish a pastoral care and counseling program among those with AIDS, I struggled. I was excited at the prospect of returning to East Africa; I had served in neighboring Tanzania for ten years and loved the people and culture of that region. But, AIDS! I hated to admit it, but I was afraid. Gradually I was able to put my fears to rest (or so I thought) and say yes to the assignment. As I approached the AIDS Unit, I realized that the fears were still there.

(Kay Lawlor)

◆ ◆ ◆ ◆ ◆

Reflect

First, to admit one's fear takes courage, and, second, more
courage is needed to overcome the fear. Unknown or
unfamiliar situations often trigger fear. But these same
unknown or unfamiliar situations can be great moments
of opportunity for personal and spiritual growth. They
can be graced opportunities for service to others. They
also can be great opportunities to experience God in new
and different ways.

Recall times in your own life when you overcame
fear in order to embrace a new experience. Who bene-
fited from such experiences? How did such experiences
help you to grow? Can you identify the source of courage
that enabled you to move into these new realities?

Respond

Loving God, grant that my mind and heart may always
be open to people and events around me, that I may find
the courage to overcome the attitudes that prevent me
from seeing things as they really are, and that I may be
able to rid myself of attitudes that keep me apart from
other people.

The Author of Authority

Listen

When they [the temple police] had brought them [the apostles], they had them stand before the council. The high priest questioned them, saying, "We gave you strict orders not to teach in this name, yet here you have filled Jerusalem with your teaching and you are determined to bring this man's blood on us." But Peter and the apostles answered, "We must obey God rather than any human authority. The God of our ancestors raised up Jesus, whom you had killed by hanging him on a tree. God exalted him at his right hand as Leader and Savior that he might give repentance to Israel and forgiveness of sins. And we are witnesses to these things, and so is the Holy Spirit whom God has given to those who obey [God]."

When they heard this, they were enraged and wanted to kill them.

(Acts of the Apostles 5:27–33)

◆ ◆ ◆ ◆ ◆

Reflect

Obeying God's will seems easier when the laws of the land accord with our beliefs about what God wants us to do. But when civil authority and obedience to God conflict, we need courage to do what Peter did—be faithful to God. To find our courage, we need to remember Peter's final sentence here, "'We are witnesses to these things, and so is the Holy Spirit whom God has given to those who obey [God].'" The Holy Spirit is not a passive observer. The Spirit in-spires, en-courages those who act in accordance with God's will.

Ask yourself, Do I have the courage to speak up, to speak out, in such situations even though it might infuriate the authorities?

Respond

God, through the heroes and heroines of the Christian Testament, you gave us impressive models of courage to guide and inspire our own actions and activities. Help me to imitate Peter by not forgetting that obedience to God is primary. Come, Holy Spirit, inspire and encourage me.

Dare to Be Different

Listen

In the mornings we do our schoolwork, in our work-books. Our mother tells us which pages to do. Then we read our school readers. Mine is about two children who live in a white house with ruffled curtains, a front lawn, and a picket fence. The father goes to work, the mother wears a dress and an apron, and the children play ball on the lawn with their dog and cat. Nothing in these stories is anything like my life. There are no tents, no highways, no peeing in the bushes, no lakes, no motels. There is no war. The children are always clean, and the little girl, whose name is Jane, wears pretty dresses and patent-leather shoes with straps.

(Margaret Atwood)

◆ ◆ ◆ ◆ ◆

Reflect

Whether we find them in a school primer or a slick tele-vision commercial, images of who we should be and what our life should be like abound. Wear the right clothes, run in the right athletic shoes, drive the right car—it is all told to us time and time again. Without courage we can easily fall prey to other people's image of how best to lead our life.

What popular images of the ideal life do you con-sciously rebel against? Is there a secret part of you that fears nonconformity with a particular societal norm that you know is bunk? What parts of your life do you value that don't correspond with current trends and popular images? Sing a defiant song against mindless conformity.

Respond

God, you did not send Jesus, Mary, and our other ances-tors in faith to preach the goodness of certain products and fulfillment according to Madison Avenue. Give me the courage that Christ may dwell in my heart through faith, so that I may be "rooted and grounded in love, . . . know the love of Christ that surpasses knowledge" and "be filled with all the fullness of God" (Ephesians 3:17–19).

Confronting Authority

Listen

On one occasion he went to the University Library to procure some books. The librarian refused to lend them. Mr. Thoreau repaired to the President, who stated to him the rules and usages, which permitted the loan of books to resident graduates, to clergymen who were alumni, and to some others resident within a circle of ten miles' radius from the College. Mr. Thoreau explained to the President that the railroad had destroyed the old scale of distances—that the library was useless, yes, and the President and College useless, on the terms of his rules—that the one benefit he owed to the College was its library—that, at this moment, not only his want of books was imperative, but he wanted a large number of books, and assured him that he, Thoreau, and not the librarian, was the proper custodian of these. In short, the President found the petitioner so formidable, and the rules getting to look so ridiculous, that he ended by giving him a privilege which in [Thoreau's] hands proved unlimited thereafter.

(Ralph Waldo Emerson)

◆ ◆ ◆ ◆ ◆

Reflect

Recall a time or two when you confronted inappropriate, stifling, or just-plain-wrong rules and regulations. Did you speak out? Were you successful? Where did you find the courage to confront this situation? Do you have situations in your life presently that you wish you had the courage to confront? What are they? How might you find the courage?

Respond

God, give me the courage to speak up and speak out. Help me to find a clear voice, a loud voice, an effective voice so that I may effect change. Help me to influence decision makers, and thereby to bring your holy presence into every aspect of our world.

Change and Changes

Listen

My father loved his farm, but he understood better than I the ironies implicit in passing on a farm in your own image. The land mocks the farmer by outlasting him and outlasting his family, no matter the number of successive generations. The one thing of permanence that a farmer can bequeath—a life of respect and respectful virtues—will be rendered ironic and pathetic if he begins to act as if he is entitled to a bailout, whether from the government or from his children. My father had to work at understanding this. It was not given. It was an achievement, like any work. I had thought of Heinrich [my great grandfather] as a pioneer, going off to a new land, and I had thought of my father as a stand-pat guy. But it was my father who had geared himself up for the bold stroke, who saw that the farm did not hold us together, as I had thought, but stood between him and his children. So he had sold it and brought us back together, or rather had gone off to find us, all of us in our own places.

(Howard Kohn)

♦ ♦ ♦ ♦ ♦

Reflect

We all experience change in our life. Sometimes the changes seem small; other times the stakes are high. Perhaps we need to find a new job. Perhaps we have to move to a new location. Perhaps a relationship has ended. Change is seldom easy.

Recall times in your life when you have summoned your courage to face major change. How did you manage? What was the ultimate outcome? What courage do you need right now to face some change?

Respond

God, you have given us lives that are ever changing. Give me the courage to live well in a changing world. Help me to befriend the revelation of change in my life and in the lives of others.

Speaking Up, Speaking Out

Listen

Jesus left that place and went away to the district of Tyre and Sidon. Just then a Canaanite woman from that region came out and started shouting, "Have mercy on me, Lord, Son of David; my daughter is tormented by a demon." But he did not answer her at all. And his disciples came and urged him, saying, "Send her away, for she keeps shouting after us." He answered, "I was sent only to the lost sheep of the house of Israel." But she came and knelt before him, saying, "Lord, help me." He answered, "It is not fair to take the children's food and throw it to the dogs." She said, "Yes, Lord, yet even the dogs eat the crumbs that fall from their masters' table." Then Jesus answered her, "Woman, great is your faith! Let it be done for you as you wish." And her daughter was healed instantly.

(Matthew 15:21–28)

◆ ◆ ◆ ◆ ◆

Reflect

This woman did not take no for an answer. She was willing to make her point by continuing the conversation even though it seemed perhaps futile. She did not give in to discouragement or depression at being initially rebuked and subsequently insulted. Her courage taught Jesus to expand his own mission, and today it teaches us worthwhile lessons.

In what events of your own life have you resembled this courageous Canaanite woman? Do you need to be a bit more persistent with God about any issue in your life?

Respond

God, grant us the courage to be persistent for the good of others, especially for people who are powerless, sick, or victims of discrimination. Help us to become like the Canaanite woman who did not easily give up. And grace us with the vision of Jesus who, through the Canaanite woman, expanded his own boundaries to be able to minister to everyone.

An Everyday Messiah

Listen

"The struggle to survive will begin here, in this room, where we are sitting. Whether or not the Messiah comes doesn't matter; we'll manage without him. It is because it is too late that we are commanded to hope. We shall be honest and humble and strong, and then he will come, he will come every day, thousands of times every day. He will have no face, because he will have a thousand faces. The Messiah isn't one man, Clara, he's all men. As long as there are men there will be a Messiah. One day you'll sing, and he will sing in you. Then for the last time, I'll want to cry. I shall cry. Without shame."

(Elie Wiesel)

◆ ◆ ◆ ◆ ◆

Reflect

It is tempting to wait for others, including God, to make things happen. It is hard to accept responsibility for things we would like to see happen. It requires courage to stop blaming other people, to stop expecting others to do what needs to be done, to stop waiting for God to set all things straight. It requires even more courage to act as we want both other people and God to act. We are the touch, voice, action, and healing of the Messiah.

Recall times in your life when you found courage to accept responsibility through action. Where were you at the time? Did you feel like a messiah? Did you want to sing? Did you want to cry?

Respond

I thank you, Yahweh, with all my heart;
I sing praise to you before the angels.
I worship at your holy temple and praise your name because of your constant love and faithfulness.

· · · · · · · · · · · · · ·

You answered me when I called to you;
you built up strength within me.

(Psalm 138:1–3)

The Courage to Learn

Listen

A student should not be embarrassed if a fellow student has understood something on the first or second time and he has not grasped it even after a number of attempts. If he is embarrassed because of this, it will turn out that he will have spent his time in the house of study without learning anything at all.

(Shulchan Aruch)

◆ ◆ ◆ ◆ ◆

Reflect

Courage begins by knowing the good. The good can be learned anywhere. In school we need to do more than simply take up space. After our schooling ends, we need to be ready to learn new things about the job we choose to pursue, the people around us, and the political issues that help determine the quality of our life. We constantly need to study God's word spoken in the Scriptures and in our experience. We need to have the courage to understand people, particularly those who are different from ourselves.

How do you learn "the good"? What do you read? Do you take time to really listen to loved ones, to opponents, to anyone from whom you can learn?

Respond

God of all wisdom, may I learn the good wherever it may be found and keep in mind your word:

For wisdom is a kindly spirit,

. . . .

the spirit of the Lord has filled the world.

(Wisdom of Solomon 1:6–7)

Leading Courageously

Listen

The task of future Christian leaders is not to make a little contribution to the solution of the pains and tribulations of their time, but to identify and announce the ways in which Jesus is leading God's people out of slavery, through the desert to a new land of freedom. Christian leaders have the arduous task of responding to personal struggles, family conflicts, national calamities, and international tensions with an articulate faith in God's real presence. They have to say "no" to every form of fatalism, defeatism, accidentalism or incidentalism which make people believe that statistics are telling us the truth. They have to say "no" to every form of despair in which human life is seen as a pure matter of good or bad luck. They have to say "no" to sentimental attempts to make people develop a spirit of resignation or stoic indifference in the face of the unavoidability of pain, suffering, and death.

(Henri J. M. Nouwen)

◆ ◆ ◆ ◆ ◆

Reflect

To believe in God, to articulate faith in God's real presence, to say no to despair and sentimental resignation, take courage. Yet we are called to leadership, and the courageous among us answer this call.

Recall times when you answered a call to leadership—remember, you don't have to look for dramatic, public examples. What role did your faith play in your actions? What were some courageous moments in the process of leadership for you?

Respond

May I be strengthened by your word, God my light:

Those who serve God
    must be ready to be tested.
Set your heart in the right direction
    and be strong.
In times of disaster, do not weaken.
Gold is always tested in fire.
Trust God, and God will help you.
Hold firm to the good, and hope in God.
                                (Adapted from Sirach 2:1–6)

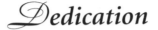

Dedication

Listen

Now there was a woman who had been suffering from hemorrhages for twelve years; and though she had spent all she had on physicians, no one could cure her. She came up behind [Jesus] and touched the fringe of his clothes, and immediately her hemorrhage stopped. Then Jesus asked, "Who touched me?" When all denied it, Peter said, "Master, the crowds surround you and press in on you." But Jesus said, "Someone touched me; for I noticed that power had gone out from me." When the woman saw that she could not remain hidden, she came trembling; and falling down before him, she declared in the presence of all the people why she had touched him, and how she had been immediately healed. He said to her, "Daughter, your faith has made you well; go in peace."

(Luke 8:43–48)

◆ ◆ ◆ ◆ ◆

Reflect

It is amazing to think of a person who after twelve years of sickness still has the courage to actively seek out a cure for her illness. As Jesus remarks though, her faith made her well. Faith manifests itself in courageous action.

How do you find the courage to keep searching for things that are important to you? Do you find yourself touching the fringe of Christ's cloak in difficult times? Can you see times in your life when your own courage has eventually won the day? Give thanks for those acts of courage, and ask for the faith to keep searching.

Respond

God, grant me the courage to avoid discouragement and to keep searching for your healing presence. I pray especially for the sick who, in their search for healing, are courageous in their faith in you. Grant them peace of mind, health of spirit, and cure of illness.

The First Martyr

Listen

But filled with the Holy Spirit, [Stephen] gazed into
heaven and saw the glory of God and Jesus standing at
the right hand of God. "Look," he said, "I see the heavens
opened and the Son of Man standing at the right hand of
God!" But they covered their ears, and with a loud shout
all rushed together against him. Then they dragged him
out of the city and began to stone him; and the witnesses
laid their coats at the feet of a young man named Saul.
While they were stoning Stephen, he prayed, "Lord Jesus,
receive my spirit." Then he knelt down and cried out in
a loud voice, "Lord, do not hold this sin against them."
When he had said this, he died.

(Acts of the Apostles 7:55–60)

Reflect

Imagine the courage of this first martyr. No other Christian believers had yet died for their beliefs. Stephen was the first. His efforts are remembered in the church calendar by placing his feast day immediately after Christmas. But there have been legions of martyrs since Stephen, women and men who have had their life taken for their faith: Agatha, Lucy, Jean Donovan, Peter, Paul, Oscar Romero, and on and on. Then there are martyrs who have given their own life in service to their sisters and brothers: Catherine of Siena, Louise de Marillac, Dorothy Day, Vincent de Paul, John Baptist de La Salle, Frédéric Ozanam.

What acts of love are you doing for the good of your sisters and brothers? How are you pouring out your life's energies for the good? How do you find the strength to forgive those who hurt you because of your beliefs?

Respond

Forgiving God, Stephen followed the example of Christ by his own death and by forgiving those who persecuted him. Help me also to find the courage to forgive those who attempt to silence my efforts to give witness to your mighty deeds and boundless love.

Acknowledgments *(continued)*

The psalms in this book are from *Psalms Anew: In Inclusive Language*, compiled by Nancy Schreck and Maureen Leach (Winona, MN: Saint Mary's Press, 1986). Copyright © 1986 by Saint Mary's Press. All rights reserved.

The scriptural quotations on pages 58 and 83 are freely adapted and are not to be interpreted or used as official translations of the Scriptures.

All other scriptural quotations in this book are from the New Revised Standard Version of the Bible. Copyright © 1989 by the Division of Christian Education of the National Council of the Churches of Christ in the United States of America. All rights reserved.

The excerpt on page 8 by Bayazid is quoted from *The Song of the Bird*, by Anthony de Mello (New York: Image Books, 1982), page 153. Copyright © 1982 by Anthony de Mello, SJ.

The excerpt on page 11 by Vincent de Paul is from *La Vie du Venerable Serviteur de Dieu Vincent de Paul*, by Louis Abelly (Paris: Florentin Lambert, 1664), pages 177–178.

The excerpt on pages 11–12 by Teresa of Ávila is from *The Book of Her Life*, in *The Collected Works of St. Teresa of Ávila*, translated by Kieran Kavanaugh and Otilio Rodriguez (Washington, DC: ICS Publications, 1976), page 137.

The excerpt on page 14 is from *The Awakened Heart*, by Gerald May (New York: HarperCollins Publishers, 1991), page 110. Copyright © 1991 by Gerald May.

The excerpt on page 20 is from *Taking Flight: A Book of Story Meditations*, by Anthony de Mello, SJ (New York: Doubleday, 1988), page 159. Copyright © 1988 by Gujarat Sahitya Prakash.

The excerpt on pages 22–23 by Eleanor Roosevelt is from *You Learn by Living*, 1960, as quoted in *Familiar Quotations*, by John Bartlett, edited by Emily Morison Beck (Boston: Little, Brown and Company, 1980), page 786. Copyright © 1980 by Little, Brown and Company.

The excerpt on page 23 by Rollo May is from *Man's Search for Himself* (New York: W. W. Norton and Company, 1953), page 160. Copyright © 1953 by W. W. Norton and Company.

The excerpt on page 24 about Jackie Robinson is from *Fresh Packet of Sower's Seeds: Third Planting*, by Brian Cavanaugh, TOR (Mahwah, NJ: Paulist Press, 1994), pages 55–56. Copyright © 1994 by Brian Cavanaugh.

Titles in the Life in Abundance series

Growing in Courage by Peter Gilmour
Growing in Hope by Lou Anne M. Tighe
Growing in Joy by Robert F. Morneau

Order from your local bookstore or from
Saint Mary's Press
702 Terrace Heights
Winona, MN 55987-1320
USA
1-800-533-8095

Jesus said . . . "I came that [you] may have life, and have it
abundantly." (John 10:10)

Jesus' mission is accomplished in each one of us when we nourish
the seeds of full life that God has planted in the garden of our soul.